Harriet Tubman

A Woman of

COURAGE

By the Editors of TIME For Kids
WITH RENÉE SKELTON

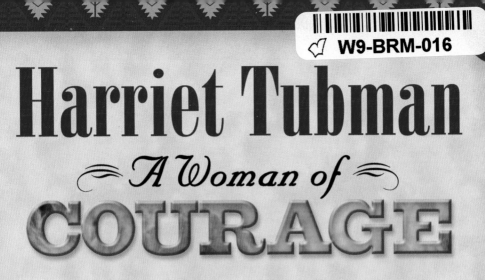

HarperCollins*Publishers*

About the Author: Renée Skelton often writes about America's past. She has a special interest in the development of our nation's history and culture, and the people who played an important part in its formation. Ms. Skelton is based in a historic town on the coast of New Jersey.

Harriet Tubman

Copyright © 2005 by Time Inc.

Used under exclusive license by HarperCollins Publishers Inc.

Manufactured in China by South China Printing Company Ltd.

Library of Congress cataloging-in-publication data is available.

ISBN 0-06-057607-3 (pbk.)—ISBN 0-06-057608-1 (trade)

14 15 SCP 20 19 18 17 16 15 14 13

First Edition

Photography and Illustration Credits:
Cover: Janice Huse; cover inset: Raymond Dobard; cover flap: Bettmann–Corbis; table of contents: Janice Huse; title page: Eileen McHugh–Cayuga Museum of History; p.iv: Corbis; p.2 (top): Library of Congress; pp.2–3 (bottom): Hulton Archive–Getty Images; p.4: Florida State Archives; p.5: Kathryn Hewitt; p.6: Hulton Archive–Getty Images; p.7: Library of Congress; p.8: Library of Congress; p.9 (both images): Library of Congress; p.10: Janice Huse; p.11: Janice Huse; p.12: Hulton Archive–Getty Images; p.13: Janice Huse; p.14: Library of Congress; p.15: TIME FOR KIDS; pp.16–17: Janice Huse; p.18: Ohio Historical Society; p.19: Janice Huse; p.20: Janice Huse; p.21: Ohio Historical Society; p.22: Library of Congress; p.23: Janice Huse; p.24: Kathryn Hewitt; p.25: National Archives; p.26: Raymond Dobard; p.27 (top): Library of Congress; p.27 (bottom): Raymond Dobard; p.28: Corbis; p.29: Corbis; p.30: Library of Congress; p.31: Minnesota Historical Society–Corbis; pp.32–33: Corbis; p.33 (bottom): Janice Huse; p.34: courtesy The Harriet Tubman Home, Inc; p.35 (top): Bettmann–Corbis; p.35 (bottom): Culver Pictures, Inc; p.36–37 (top): public domain; p.36 (bottom): Bettmann–Corbis; p.37: courtesy Chris Mercogliano–The Free School; p.38 (top corner left): Eileen McHugh–Cayuga Museum of History; pp.38–39 (top middle): Janice Huse; p.39 (bottom): courtesy Washington College; p.40: public domain; p.41: Library of Congress; p.42: courtesy Christine King Farris; pp.42–43 (bottom): Time Life Pictures–Getty Images; p.43 (top): Brand X–Getty Images; p.44 (top to bottom): Massachusetts Historical Society; Hulton Archive by Getty Images; Photodisc; Time Life Pictures–Getty Images; back cover: Corbis

Acknowledgments:
For TIME FOR KIDS: Editorial Director: Keith Garton; Editor: Jonathan Rosenbloom; Art Director: Rachel Smith; Photography Editor: Sandy Perez

go Find out more at www.timeforkids.com/bio/tubman

CONTENTS

▶ STANDING PROUD
This is one of the few photos ever taken of Harriet Tubman. She posed for it in Auburn, New York.

≈ *A Woman of* ≈
COURAGE

Harriet Tubman was born a slave. But she made up her mind that she would not die a slave. With courage and determination, Tubman bravely won her own freedom—and the freedom of hundreds of other slaves.

When she died at the age of ninety-three, Harriet Tubman was a famous and respected American. The former slave risked her life many times to help other people become free. She also served her country during the Civil War as a spy and a scout. In her later years she opened her

> *"I had reasoned this out in my mind. There was one of two things I had a right to—liberty or death. If I could not have one, I would have the other."*
>
> —HARRIET TUBMAN

◀ **SLAVE SHIPS** carried people from Africa to the United States. The trip was terrible, with little food, water, or air.

home to people in need— asking nothing for herself in return.

No one knows exactly when Harriet was born. It was probably around 1820 in Bucktown, Maryland. Slave traders had captured Harriet's grandparents in West Africa. Her parents,

Harriet Green and Benjamin Ross, were born as slaves. So when Harriet and her brothers and sisters were born, they were slaves, too. Her parents named her Araminta. But people called her by her mother's name, Harriet.

A Hard Life

Harriet, her parents, and her ten brothers and sisters lived and worked on the Brodess plantation near Bucktown. A plantation was a large farm where

▼ SLAVES WORKED long hours. Here, a group of slaves is working in a plantation field.

slaves did all the work. Because Harriet was a slave, her childhood was much more work than play. She started to work when she was just five years old. She was hired out to a nearby plantation to care for the owner's baby. When she was six, she learned to weave and make clothes. As a young teen, she labored in the fields of corn, potatoes, and tobacco. Harriet was strong. She was very good at her jobs. But Harriet was also independent and rebellious in nature. This made her owners very angry. They would punish her with beatings.

Helping Others

When she was thirteen, Harriet's independence got her into real trouble. One evening she was harvesting crops with a group of other slaves. One of the men left to go to the village store. Because he didn't have permission, the overseer followed him. (An overseer was a person who was in charge of the slaves.) Harriet followed, too. When the overseer caught up with the man, he threatened to whip him. The overseer told Harriet to help him hold the man down. She refused. It made Harriet very angry to see people beaten. In the confusion the man tried to run away. As the overseer tried to stop him, Harriet blocked the way. The overseer picked up a heavy weight and threw it at the man. But it hit Harriet in the head instead. Part of her skull was crushed, and she crumpled to the ground.

It took a very long time for Harriet to feel better. For the rest of her life, she had blackouts because of the injury. Harriet would suddenly fall into

COURAGE AT AN EARLY AGE
Harriet always wanted to help others. Even as a teen, she stood up to adults. ▲

a deep sleep for a period of time. Then she would wake up just as suddenly and go on as though nothing had happened.

▶ A SLAVE FAMILY sits outside their cabin around the year 1860.

After Harriet became strong enough to work again, she went back to the fields. She drove oxen. She plowed the ground. She chopped wood and carried logs. She could do just about any job a man could do. She also learned a lot about the woods from her father—information that would come in handy later in life.

Harriet learned something else as well. She saw friends and family members work all day from sunrise

SLAVE

▲ SLAVE CHILDREN worked from early morning to nighttime. They had little time for play and they didn't go to school.

hildren began to work when they were young—usually five or six years old. They'd start out looking after younger children, running errands, gathering firewood, or helping with planting. As they got older, they would get more and harder work to do. By the time they were twelve, some children started to work in the fields. They would rake, hoe, clear weeds, and pick crops such as cotton. Some

until sunset. She saw them cruelly beaten. Harriet hated slavery, and she began to dream of a different life for herself and her family.

CHILDREN

children also learned skills, such as weaving or cooking.

Like all slaves, children were property that could be sold at any time. Families were separated when slave owners sold a parent or a child. This is how one former slave remembered childhood:

"My owners hired me out to some people that lived in the country. I was only about six years old.... I had to nurse, cook, work in the fields, chop wood, bring water, wash, and do everything....

"Every morning I was up at five o'clock. I slept [on a mat] in the corner every night.... After dressing, I made the fires, milked two cows, drove them to the pastures, and came back and brought water from the spring for the house. Then I helped with breakfast, and went to the field to work."

Making Her Way
ALONE

When Harriet was in her twenties, much of her life changed. She married John Tubman, a free African American man who lived near the plantation. But when Harriet married John, she didn't become free, too. Under the law she was still a slave. So she still had to work for the family who owned her. The only change was that Harriet was allowed to spend nights at her husband's cabin.

Harriet wondered how long she and her

▲ HOLDING ROOMS
Slaves were kept in jail-like cells before they were sold off in auctions.

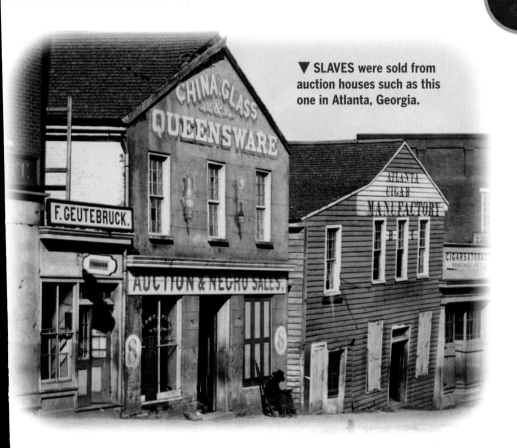

▼ SLAVES were sold from auction houses such as this one in Atlanta, Georgia.

husband would be together. After all, the owner of the plantation could sell her at any time. Harriet had heard rumors that the owner was going to do just that.

The rumors upset Harriet very much. She wanted to stay with her family. She told John she wanted to run away from the

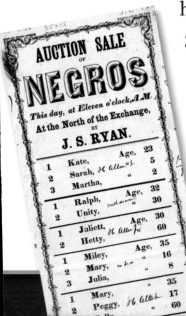

AUCTION SALE
OF
NEGROS
This day, at Eleven o'clock, A.M.
At the North of the Exchange,
BY
J. S. RYAN.

		Age,	
1	Kate,		23
2	Sarah, H. Allway,	"	5
3	Martha,	"	2
1	Ralph,	Age,	32
2	Unity,	"	30
1	Juliett, H. Allway,	Age,	30
2	Hetty,		60
1	Miley,	Age,	35
2	Mary,	"	16
3	Julia,	"	8
1	Mary,		35
2	Peggy, H. Allway,	"	17
			60

◀ SLAVE AUCTIONS were held throughout the slave states. In the days of slavery, and later, African Americans were called Negroes.

▶ HARRIET TRIED to convince her husband to escape to the North. He decided not to go. So Harriet went without him.

Brodess plantation. She was eager to go north and be free. Most northern states did not allow slavery. If a slave escaped to one of those states, he or she became free. But John Tubman didn't like the idea. It would be dangerous. Also, there was a good chance that they'd be caught and beaten. He told Harriet to forget about leaving.

Harriet stopped talking to her husband about her plan. But she didn't forget about it. In fact, the more she thought about it, the more Harriet knew that she wanted to leave. She wanted to go with her husband. But if he refused to go, she would seek her freedom alone.

Planning the Escape

By 1849 Harriet was sure that she would soon be sold to another owner far away—and farther away from the North. Harriet knew she had to leave before it was too late. She didn't tell her husband she was going, because she thought he would try to stop her. Instead, she got in touch with people who lived outside the plantation and could help her. She secretly made her plans to escape.

One night Harriet and two of her brothers snuck out of their cabins. They ran into the nearby woods and followed a path away from the plantation. But before long Harriet's brothers changed their minds. They knew how difficult it would be to get away. They knew they would be beaten if they were caught. So the two men decided to go back before someone came looking for them. But Harriet refused to return. She told them she would go on by herself.

Without her brothers to help and protect her, Harriet was afraid. She was a young woman, alone in the forest. How would she get food? And how did someone get to the North anyway? She really didn't know the way.

▶ AFRAID BUT DETERMINED, Harriet sets out by herself for the free northern state of Pennsylvania. Her brothers turned back because they were afraid they'd be caught.

On the Way to
FREEDOM

Harriet had directions to the house of a woman who would help on the first part of her journey. But Harriet didn't know this person. Could it be a trap? What if the slave hunters were waiting for her there? She could imagine the beating she would get from her owner if she were dragged back. Harriet tried to forget her fears as she walked on.

Harriet reached the home of the woman who promised to help her. As it turns out, she did not have to worry.

▲ SAFE HOUSES like this one offered escaping slaves a place to hide. The houses were stations on the Underground Railroad.

The kind woman was part of the Underground Railroad, a network of people who helped slaves escape.

Harriet was tired, thirsty, and very hungry. The woman gave her food and water. Then she told Harriet to climb into a waiting wagon. Harriet lay down, hidden by a burlap bag and vegetables, and then she was driven to another secret location. These kind people helped Harriet and many other slaves find freedom.

Follow Your Star

When Harriet was lucky, she got rides for short distances. But most of the time she walked. She took lonely back roads and sheltered paths through the woods by night, following the North Star. Along the

way strangers who were part of the Underground Railroad network helped her. Sometimes they gave Harriet food and hid her during the day. Then they gave her directions to the next place where she could get help. She crossed from Maryland into Delaware. Then she walked north into the free state of Pennsylvania.

Harriet walked almost one hundred miles from her

THE UNDERGROUND

The Underground Railroad wasn't a *real* railroad with tracks and trains. It was a network of people and routes—on land and water—that helped slaves escape from the South in the mid-1800s.

Thousands of people in cities, villages, and farm areas of the United States, Canada, and Mexico were part of the network.

Between 30,000 and 100,000 slaves escaped to freedom on the "Railroad" between the 1830s and the end of the Civil War.

"Conductors" were people who helped the runaways. "Stations" were places such as overgrown areas in forests or attics or cellars in houses where slaves could hide. Conductors gave escaping slaves food, shelter, and clothing. They also helped the slaves get to the next station. At night conductors snuck the slaves out of their hiding places. Most of them went on

◀ HARRIET WALKED to the big city of Philadelphia, Pennsylvania. This is how Philadelphia looked in the mid-1800s.

home to freedom in Pennsylvania. Then she headed for Philadelphia. She got a job there as a dishwasher and cook. Harriet also met abolitionists—people who wanted to end the practice of slavery.

The abolitionists told her many details about how the Underground Railroad worked. This helped Harriet as she began the greatest adventures of her life.

RAILROAD LEGEND

foot, although some traveled in wagons, sleighs, and boats.

Most conductors on the Underground Railroad were African Americans who lived in the North. But whites and others became part of the network, too. The conductors took great risks to help escaping slaves. If they were found out, the conductors could lose their jobs.

And if escaping slaves were caught, they'd be dragged back to their owners and punished.

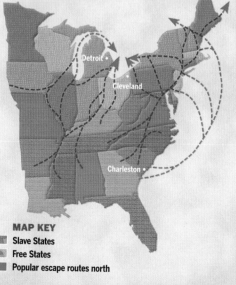

▼ ROUTES TO FREEDOM
The dotted lines show the escape routes of the Underground Railroad.

MAP KEY
▪ Slave States
▪ Free States
▪ Popular escape routes north

~ Working on the ~
RAILROAD

Harriet loved being free. For the first time in her life, people paid her for her work. She had her own place to live. She could come and go as she pleased. But she thought about her family a lot. She missed them and wanted them to be free. She wanted them to be with her.

In 1850 Harriet decided to go back to Maryland to free her family. Her decision took great courage because she was a runaway slave. Once Harriet

▲ A GROUP of slaves runs away from the plantation. Next stop? Freedom!

returned to Maryland, anyone could capture her and force her back into slavery.

A Dangerous Journey

Harriet returned to the Brodess plantation, where she had lived, and took the first members of her family north—a sister and her children. They walked by night and hid by day. Along the way conductors of the Underground Railroad helped them. Harriet made several trips back to Maryland over the next few years. On one trip she went back for her husband, but he had married someone else and did not want to leave. However, Harriet brought many of her brothers and sisters and their families north to freedom.

Harriet became famous for her work as a conductor on the Underground Railroad. She helped her family, and she helped many others, too. Harriet made nineteen trips to the South between 1850 and 1860 to lead three hundred slaves to freedom. In the 1850s, Maryland slave owners offered rewards that added up to $40,000 for her

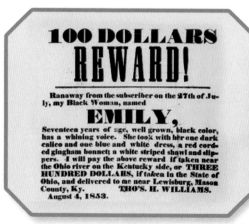

100 DOLLARS REWARD!

Ranaway from the subscriber on the 27th of July, my Black Woman, named

EMILY,

Seventeen years of age, well grown, black color, has a whining voice. She took with her one dark calico and one blue and white dress, a red corded gingham bonnet; a white striped shawl and slippers. I will pay the above reward if taken near the Ohio river on the Kentucky side, or THREE HUNDRED DOLLARS, if taken in the State of Ohio, and delivered to me near Lewisburg, Mason County, Ky. THO'S. H. WILLIAMS. August 4, 1853.

▲ SLAVE OWNERS offered rewards to find and return runaway slaves. This notice is for a slave named Emily.

capture. No one ever caught her.

Bringing slaves to freedom was dangerous and hard. Once owners discovered that a slave was missing, men with guns went out to search for the runaway. The slave hunters patrolled the roads and searched buildings. Slaves who were caught were severely punished. Most slaves tried several times before they finally reached freedom. Some never made it at all.

Runaway slaves and the people who helped them had to be clever to avoid capture. First they tried to get

▲ SLAVES HAD TO HIDE from slave hunters. They often found shelter and food in Underground Railroad stations.

a long head start when they escaped. That meant escaping when slave owners wouldn't miss them right away.

Most slaves escaped on a holiday or a weekend. Harriet often took slaves away from plantations on a Saturday night. Most slaves did not have to work on Sundays. So their owners wouldn't miss them and start searching until Monday.

It was important to keep plans and movements secret. Escaping slaves usually traveled at night. During the day they hid in the woods and fields or other shelters the people of the Underground Railroad provided. Sometimes Harriet would hide her "passengers," then check to see if it was safe for them to come out to get food, clothing, or rest at a station on the way. She might knock at the door of a house that was known as a station on the Underground Railroad. Perhaps the person inside would ask, "Who is there?" Then Harriet might answer, "A friend with a friend." That would let the person know that she had runaway slaves with her. Once she knew the way was clear, Harriet returned with her passengers.

Playing Tricks

Runaways did what they could to trick people who hunted them. Slave hunters often tracked slaves with dogs. The dogs' sharp sense of smell helped them find the slaves. The slaves sometimes poured pepper on the trail to confuse the dogs or walked through water to hide their scent. Some slaves didn't head north right away. They hid near home until the people who were looking for them thought they were long gone and stopped looking. Then the slaves would start their journey.

◀ **THOUSANDS OF SLAVES** climbed these stairs in Ripley, Ohio, to a safe house on the Underground Railroad.

A Tough
LEADER

Harriet Tubman succeeded because she was a very tough leader. Once she started north with a group of passengers, no one was allowed to turn back. She knew that slaves who turned back might get caught. Then officials might force them to give away the location of other runaways and people who helped them. So Harriet always carried a gun with her. If someone thought he or she couldn't

▲ **ON TRACK TO FREEDOM**
Sometimes trains were used by Underground Railroad conductors to help slaves escape.

▲ **SLAVES CELEBRATE THEIR FREEDOM** as they finally reach safety in the North.

go on, she said she'd shoot. She never did. But her words were enough to make people continue.

Harriet and her passengers had many close calls. On one rescue trip slave hunters were close behind her. They caught up with her and her passengers near a train station. Harriet had to think fast. She quickly pushed her passengers onto a train heading south. She knew the slave hunters would never look on that train. After all, runaway slaves wanted to go north, not south. The trick worked perfectly and the authorities paid no attention to them.

Rescue Mission

On another mission Harriet was back in Bucktown, Maryland, to pick up the members of her family. She had just bought some live chickens at the market when she suddenly saw her former owner walking toward her. If he saw her, her days as a free woman were over. She quickly dropped the chickens. As they squawked and flapped their wings on the ground, she turned her back and bent over to catch them. Her former owner walked right past her.

In 1857 Harriet made her most difficult journey—to get her parents. By this time they were old and could not walk very far. Harriet had to drive them in a wagon through the states of Maryland and Delaware. A big wagon was difficult to hide and made it more likely that someone would stop them. But, despite this, Harriet succeeded. She brought her parents

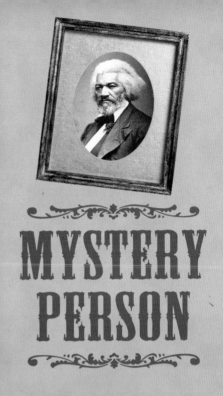

MYSTERY PERSON

CLUE 1: This man lived from 1818(?) to 1895. As a slave child he had learned to read, even though it was forbidden. When he was twenty years old, he escaped from slavery.

CLUE 2: This man went on to publish the antislavery newspaper *North Star*. He helped hundreds of slaves find their way to freedom.

CLUE 3: Later in his life he became a good friend of Harriet Tubman. He was also a great stationmaster on the Underground Railroad.

Can you name this man?

Answer: Frederick Douglass

from Maryland all the way to freedom in Canada, where she had been living. The family then moved to the small town of Auburn, in upstate New York. Harriet and her parents settled in a small house where they all lived together.

Harriet made her last trip south before the Civil War in December of 1860. She brought seven people north to freedom. Harriet Tubman was among the

THE SECRET QUILT

Most slaves could not read and write. In fact, it was against the law for anyone to teach them. So they came up with clever ways to share information about escape plans. They passed messages in songs and even on quilts.

It wasn't unusual to see quilts hanging out windows or lying across fences to air out. So the quilts didn't stir up suspicion from slave owners. The patterns on the quilts often held messages that told escaping slaves when to get ready, when to leave, and where to go.

greatest leaders known from the Underground Railroad. She was very proud. "I never lost one passenger," she said.

ODE AND PATCHES *that* POINTED *the* WAY

▼ FLYING GEESE
Since geese fly north in the spring, this pattern gave fleeing slaves two important instructions: Head north, and travel in the spring.

▲ DRUNKARD'S PATH
This pattern held a helpful warning: Slaves were to travel in a zigzag pattern in order to avoid leaving a clear path for slave catchers to follow.

▲ NORTH STAR
This popular quilt design is also known as the Star or the Evening Star. In code, escaping slaves were told to follow the North Star.

The Civil War YEARS

By 1860 Harriet Tubman was well known for her daring slave rescues. She made speeches against slavery at abolitionist meetings. She also spoke to support the struggle for women's rights. During Harriet's lifetime, women did not have the same rights as men.

Harriet's life was about to change once again. In early 1861 a huge problem was growing in the United States. The slave states and the free states disagreed about

▲ **UNION SOLDIERS** stand at attention in this photo. It was taken during the Civil War.

▲ A CONFEDERATE FLAG rises over Fort Sumter the day after the surrender.

whether slavery should be allowed in the new western territories. Abraham Lincoln was against the spread of slavery to the West. So when he became president in November 1860, the slave states feared that he would end slavery. Eleven southern slave states separated from the United States. They formed a separate country called the Confederate States of America. In April 1861 Confederate soldiers attacked the Union's Fort Sumter in South Carolina. The Civil War had begun.

A Hard Decision

▲ WHAT'S COOKING?
A battlefield kitchen during
the Civil War was usually a
group of big pots over a fire.

When the Civil War started, Harriet helped the Union. It was a hard decision for Harriet. Her parents lived with her and she took care of them. Who would care for them if she left? Finally Harriet decided that she had to go. The cause of the Union was too important. When Harriet was gone, people in Auburn helped care for her mother and father.

During the Civil War, Harriet did many jobs to help others. She worked as a nurse and cook for the Union. Harriet was also a valuable scout and spy. She knew how to survive in forests and swamps. She often went behind enemy lines in the South and gained the trust of slaves there. They gave her important information about the location of Confederate supplies and Confederate soldiers. She took that information to the Union army. Harriet also led a group of former slaves who spied on the Confederate States.

This brave woman also led Union soldiers through enemy territory as a scout. In 1863 she led a group of one hundred fifty African American soldiers on a raid up the Combahee River in South Carolina. They destroyed Confederate supplies and crops and freed about

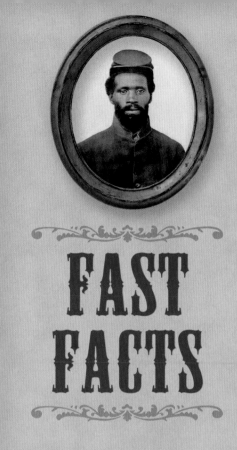

FAST FACTS

☛ Most Slaves escaped to northern states or Canada on the Underground Railroad. But some went to Mexico, the Caribbean islands, and territories in the West.

☛ A group of African Americans who had escaped slavery started a settlement on the west coast of Africa in 1822. It became the country of Liberia in 1847.

☛ About 134,000 freed slaves fought for the Union during the Civil War.

SINGING FOR FREEDOM

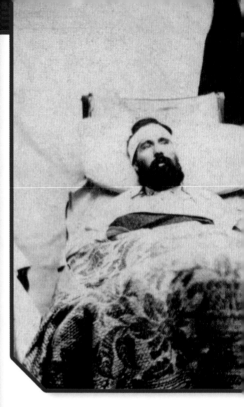

The words of songs were sometimes a code that gave instructions to slaves. The words to "Follow the Drinking Gourd" told slaves about an escape route from Alabama and Mississippi. Here are some of the words:

The riverbank makes a very good road. The dead trees show you the way. Left foot, peg foot, traveling on. Follow the drinking gourd.

The song told slaves to follow the banks of a local river and look for dead trees along the way. The trees were marked with drawings of a left foot and a peg foot. The Drinking Gourd was the Big Dipper, which the slaves used to find the North Star. They followed the North Star to freedom.

eight hundred slaves.

Harriet worked in army hospitals. She took care of hurt soldiers. She bathed them and cleaned their wounds. Some of her homemade remedies, made from local plants and roots, helped ease the fever and suffering of sick soldiers.

Harriet also baked pies and gingerbread and made root beer at night

in her tiny cabin. A friend sold the goodies at army camps to help Harriet support herself since she didn't get a salary from the army for her work.

When the Civil War ended in 1865, Harriet returned to her home in Auburn, New York. During the four-year struggle, she had helped in the fight to keep the Union together—and to end slavery. She had helped make the lives of sick and wounded soldiers a bit better. She had risked her life to fight for freedom for all people. But Harriet knew that there was still much more work to be done.

Now it was time to help others closer to home.

▶ IMPORTANT MISSION
Harriet often passed on information she had learned from slaves to Union spies.

Harriet's Later YEARS

Harriet was happy to be back home in Auburn with her parents. But Harriet was poor. She had spent her whole life helping others, and she had very little money. After the war the U.S. government wouldn't give her money for her work during the war. She still owed money to a bank for the house she shared with her mother and father. Now the bank said they would take Harriet's house if she could not pay back the money she owed them.

▲ **THE TUBMAN HOUSE** became a home for elderly African Americans who had nowhere else to live.

▲ **HARRIET TUBMAN** (far left) is shown with a group of slaves she helped to escape.

A writer named Sarah Bradford heard about Harriet's problem. Sarah admired Harriet for her courage and hard work. Harriet had helped many people, and now Sarah wanted to help her. Harriet agreed to let Sarah write a book about her life. The book told the amazing story of Harriet's escape from slavery and her work on the Underground Railroad. It was published in 1869. The book was very popular, and

▶ **HARRIET TUBMAN** posed for this photograph while living in Auburn, New York.

► AN AMAZING TALE TO TELL
This book was written by Sarah Bradford.
It tells the story of Harriet Tubman's life.

HARRIET TUBMAN.

Bradford shared the money she made from it with Harriet. This income helped pay Harriet's debts and saved the Tubman house.

Happy Event!

In 1870 another happy event in Harriet's life took place. She married Nelson Davis. She had met him during the Civil War, while she was guiding a group of black soldiers in South Carolina. He was a former slave who had joined the Union army. They were together for eighteen years, until his death in 1888.

◄ BRADFORD shared her profits from her book with Harriet. This is what the dollar looked like in the late 1800s.

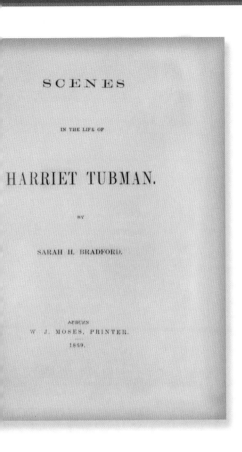

PAYING UP

More than thirty years after the Civil War ended, the army finally gave Harriet some of the money she deserved. She was given twenty dollars each month, starting in 1897. But that wasn't for the work she did during the war. It was the money the government owed to

In 2002 a group of students from the Free School in Albany, New York, visited stops along the Underground Railroad. The kids learned that Harriet Tubman never got her full Civil War pension from the U.S. government.

The kids spoke to Senator Hillary Clinton of New York. Clinton got Congress to give $11,750 to the Tubman home in Auburn. The money was used to buy furniture from Harriet's time so visitors to the house can see it. The students helped correct an injustice the government committed more than one hundred years ago.

HARRIET BY THE NUMBERS

5 Age at which she started her first job

19 Number of times she went south to lead slaves to freedom

29 Age at which she escaped slavery

300 Approximate number of slaves she led to freedom

800 Approximate number of slaves she helped free in Civil War raids

40,000 Number of dollars slaveholders offered for her capture in the late 1850s

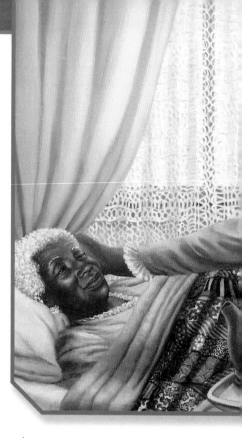

▲ **HARRIET CARED** about the health and happiness of others. She often took in older people and nursed them.

her husband, who had been a soldier.

Although Harriet didn't have much money, she always shared what she had with people who were less fortunate. Harriet took many people who were old, sick, and poor into her

home. She cared for them, but her small home didn't have a lot of space.

Harriet needed a larger building so she could help more people. In 1896 she used her small savings to buy twenty-five acres of land next to her house. There she helped create a home to care for elderly African Americans who had nowhere to go for help. The African Methodist Episcopal (AME) Zion Church ran the home, but Harriet worked there.

Harriet lived in her house next door until she became too old and sick to care for herself. Then she moved into the home

► A MARKER HONORS Harriet Tubman's work. Harriet is often compared to Moses, the man who led the Jewish people out of slavery in biblical times.

HARRIET TUBMAN
1820-1913
THE "MOSES OF HER PEOPLE," HARRIET TUBMAN OF THE BUCKTOWN DISTRICT FOUND FREEDOM FOR HERSELF AND SOME THREE HUNDRED OTHER SLAVES WHOM SHE LED NORTH. IN THE CIVIL WAR SHE SERVED THE UNION ARMY AS A NURSE, SCOUT AND SPY.

MARYLAND CIVIL WAR CENTENNIAL COMMISSION

for the aged so others could care for her. She died in 1913 from pneumonia, a lung disease. Harriet Tubman was ninety-three years old.

Harriet Tubman received many honors before and after her death. In 1897 Queen Victoria of Great Britain awarded her a silver medal for bravery. The medal honored all that Harriet Tubman had done to help African American slaves escape to the North and become free.

Although Harriet was not a Civil War soldier, she was buried in Auburn, New York, with full military honors. The United States government did this to honor her for all of her important work during the Civil War as a spy, a scout, a cook, and a hospital nurse. To honor her further, the people in the town of Auburn set up a plaque in her memory.

Harriet Tubman changed—and probably saved—the lives of

Harriet Tubman

▲ A LONG OVERDUE HONOR
In 1995 the United States government honored Harriet Tubman by putting her picture on a postage stamp. It shows her helping slaves escape to freedom.

hundreds of African Americans
by leading them out of slavery
to freedom. Her courage,

▲ HARRIET TUBMAN was an
old woman in this photo,
taken shortly before she died.

bravery, and dedication inspired many people
during her time. And her life continues to inspire
people today.

~ *Talking About* ~
HARRIET

Christine King Farris is the older sister of Dr. Martin Luther King Jr. He was a great civil rights leader in the 1950s and 1960s. TIME FOR KIDS editor Elizabeth Winchester spoke with Farris.

▲ Christine King Farris

Q. *As children, did you and your brother hear stories about Harriet Tubman? How do you feel she shaped history?*

A. Oh yes, we heard about her. She had quite an influence on all

▶ DR. MARTIN LUTHER KING JR. gave a speech in 1963 at a civil rights march in Washington, D.C. King talked about a time when all people would be treated equally.

African Americans. We want kids to learn that people who came before them paved the way for them to enjoy the freedom that we have today.

Q. *What qualities do Dr. Martin Luther King Jr. and Harriet Tubman have in common?*
A. They were both leaders. Leaders are people who are not afraid to take a stand for what they believe.

Q. *What would you say to kids who want to become leaders?*

A. You can dream big dreams. You can make a contribution. You can do well in school and read good books about people who made contributions. You too can become a leader and make a difference.

43

Harriet Tubman's KEY DATES

1820	Born in Bucktown, Maryland
1844	Marries John Tubman
1849	Uses the Underground Railroad to escape from slavery
1850	Makes the first of nineteen trips to the South to free slaves
1861	Begins four years of work for the Union army
1870	Marries Nelson Davis
1896	Buys land in Auburn to build the Tubman Home
1897	Receives honor from Queen Victoria for bravery
1913	Dies in Auburn, New York

1849 Gold is discovered at Sutter's Mill in California.

1893 The Happy Birthday tune is written.

1912 The *Titanic* sinks o[n] its first voyage more than 1,500 drown.